Your Auction Success
Maria Lawrance

#1 AMAZON BEST SELLING AUTHOR

AUCTION
SUCCESS

TOP 10 TIPS TO SUCCESSFULLY BUY PROPERTY @ AUCTION

BEST SELLER
#1 AMAZON
BEST SELLER

LEADING AUSTRALIAN AUCTIONEER & AGENT

MARIA LAWRANCE

PROPERTY SUCCESS SERIES

AUCTION SUCCESS: TOP 1O TIPS TO SUCCESSFULLY BUY PROPERTY AT AUCTION

Property Success is a new book series teaching Australians how to successfully purchase property with confidence. Whether you are an investor, first-time home buyer, downsizer or buying your dream home, Maria Lawrance will guide you through the process to make purchasing a property a most positive and successful experience for both buyers and sellers.

achieve your desired outcome; the tools, stories and information are provided as examples only, not as a source of legal or financial advice. You recognize that any business endeavour has inherent risk for loss of capital.

First Edition 2013 | Copyright 2013 by Maria Lawrance

Lawrance, Maria, author.

Auction Success: Top 10 Tips to Successfully Buy Property at Auction

Series: Lawrance, Maria, Property success ; 1.

Real property auctions--Australia.

House buying--Australia.

Real estate investment--Australia.

332.63240994

ISBN: 9780992417000 (paperback)

Table of Contents

Introduction

Sick and tired of going to auctions and getting beaten every time? Or are you one of these people who are so petrified of doing something wrong that you avoid them altogether? Hi, my name is Maria Lawrance and I have over 21 years' experience as one of Sydney's leading auctioneers, personally having sold over $44 million in properties in just the last 20 months alone. By the way, the average sale price in my area is currently $440,000 – so that's a lot of properties!

In this book, I want to dispel any myths that you have about buying at auction and teach you the secrets that Auctioneers do not want you to know to eliminate any fears you may have of buying at auction and get you back out there bidding and securing the property of your dreams.

I will show you why you should rush to look at auctions before you inspect anything else; the questions you need to ask; how to protect yourself so that you can bid with confidence; and how to strategize your bidding so you end up with the property. At the end of each chapter, I will give you tips to summarise my advice to you.

No stone has been left unturned in this 'no waffle' book. If you are someone who is looking to downsize, dip your toe in the property market, a serious investor or someone looking to buy their dream home, then this book is for you.

With almost every property in Sydney going to auction at the moment, this book is a 'Must Read' for the savvy property buyer to ensure that you can walk into any auction with confidence and play with a winning bidder's hand each and every time. I cannot guarantee that you will win the closing bid, but you will definitely go in there ahead of the crowd.

This system of selling has a very long history and is most unlikely to wane in the very near future. As I said, I am an Auctioneer with some 21 years' experience of conducting Auctions. I am also a Licensed Real Estate Agent and I actively list and sell properties. I don't encourage every vendor to go to Auction, but when I can see that this is beneficial to the owner, I encourage an Auction with gusto.

I can see that right now the real estate market is heating up again after a 10-year hiatus. How can I say this with confidence? Because there are more Auction listings out there than there have been for many, many years, and the current clearance rate across the major cities in Australia is coming in at 58.3% compared to only 40.41% at this time last year. Large numbers of Auction listings are usually indicative of prices rising and today property selling by Public Auction has never been more popular. As recently as 30th November 2013, there were a record number of properties, some 902, which went to the Auction block here in Sydney.

What does that mean to you, the buyer? Like it or not, if you want to buy a property, you are probably going to have to look at an Auction listing sooner or later. And, in all probability, if you like the property, you may have to attend an Auction and bid for it.

Does the thought of that fill you with dread? Well hopefully this handbook will help you navigate your way through all your fears, will alert you to all the pitfalls, and assist you in purchasing your new home, or investment, with the minimum of stress. I am going to let you in on a few trade secrets that will allow you to approach an auction property with more confidence and less trepidation.

Like I first said, I've now been auctioning homes across Sydney for the past 21 years. I've auctioned everything from tiny one bedroom apartments to sprawling acreages ripe for subdivision to magnificent mansions. Whatever the property, whatever the price, the game stays the same. And you need to know it inside out if you want to play!

CHAPTER 1

WHY SELL BY PUBLIC AUCTION?

There are really only three methods to sell a property: Private Treaty, For Sale by Tender or For Sale by Public Auction.

Private Treaty

A Private Treaty sale, simply put, involves the owner, or vendor, putting an 'asking price' on a property which is usually set at a figure with room for negotiation. Then the property will be marketed at this price and buyers that want the property will then make offers in accordance to the benchmark price that has been set. Very rarely will an owner be offered more than the asking price or even at the asking price.

Every buyer believes they are the only buyer interested in the property and seem to make it their mission to get as much as possible reduced off that asking price. They also want their terms and conditions met, such as a delayed settlement, inclusions added that were not in the contract, or a variety of terms changed. Usually these negotiations are done between the two parties through a Real Estate Agent and there will be to-ing and fro-ing until a figure and terms are agreed upon.

In today's marketplace in NSW, most agents will not take a property 'off the market' until a purchaser has signed a contract at the agreed price, or at their best offer. There are no 'holding deposits' taken. The deposit has to amount to .25% of the purchase price, or the price offered. The agent will then take this signed contract to the owner and if the owner signs the counterpart contract, both contracts are dated and sent off to the respective solicitors. This exchange is done with a cooling-off period which cannot legally be under five business days, but the cooling off time can be negotiated out further.

During this cooling off period, the owner is locked into that contract. He cannot accept a higher offer. He cannot change his mind about selling. He has to wait it out until the end of the cooling off period to see if his buyer can perform or still wants to perform. This makes the owner very vulnerable, particularly if he is buying himself and he needs the funds from his sale to complete his own purchase. If the purchaser changes his mind for any reason whatsoever, he does have to forfeit his original deposit to the owner, but often these monies are less than what the owner has to forego himself if he is upgrading to a higher price range. It is also at the end of a cool off time that a ruthless buyer can insist on a price reduction for whatever reason. An owner in a tight corner may have no choice but to comply with the reduction in price or lose the sale.

Through the Private Treaty method, there is no definite sale until the balance of the deposit monies are paid by 5 pm on the last business day of the cool off. This does leave the owner in limbo until this takes place and causes a lot of stress to most vendors. Should the sale fall through then the owner has to put the property back on the market and go through the whole agonising process again. In some unlucky instances, this may happen several times before a sale is actually finalised. By this time, most owners' nerves are totally frazzled. Unfortunately if this does happen, what can also occur is that savvy buyers see the property back on the market and get even harder with their negotiations. The owner may not have any choice but to take a lesser amount than preferred just to get the job done.

For Sale By Tender

For Sale by Tender is very similar to the Auction process except that buyers' bids are not disclosed to each other. A date will be set for buyers to submit their best offer and terms and then the vendor will accept what he considers to be his best offer and terms. The successful bidder is then notified. You are not given a second chance to bid for the property. If your bid isn't the winning bid, you cannot improve on it. However, often these offers are still submitted with a cooling-off contract and the sale is still not unconditional at the point of the owner accepting the offer. Again, the vendor is in a vulnerable position.

For Sale By Public Auction

With a sale by Public Auction, once the hammer comes down, the property is sold. No cooling-off contract, a definite sale at a definite price, no further negotiations. Obviously this is very powerful and favours the vendor more than the buyer. Buyers are at liberty to bid to whatever price they deem the property to be worth. The competition is no longer to drive the owner's price down but to beat another buyer for the property. The terms and conditions of purchasing the property are in the Contract for Sale and these have to be adhered to by the buyer (unless their solicitor has made requests prior to the auction). All in all, this system puts the owner back in the driving seat, rather than the other way around.

Then, of course, there is the matter of price. With all the media attention that the real estate market gets, we are constantly hearing about properties selling well over the reserve price and how hot the market is. It's only natural that a homeowner needing to sell in these conditions wants a piece of that action. Every owner hopes that there will be spirited bidding at his Auction and that he can end up with more money than he was anticipating. Some of the figures being reached above the reserve price are similar to winning Lotto! Sometimes this does happen, sometimes it doesn't. Remember: the clearance rate under the hammer across Australia this year sits at 58.3% - there's still 41.7% of stock where the reserve price hasn't been met and those properties didn't sell.

The most popular properties are generally the ones going to Auction. They can be popular because of their presentation, location, or potential for further development or a combination of these reasons.

Deceased Estates

Will also more than likely go to Auction. Usually this is recommended by the solicitor dealing with the Estate simply because a Public Auction can avoid conflict between beneficiaries and should bring the very best price. A beneficiary has less argument to dispute that figure with a Public Auction.

Mortgagee in Possession sales

Are mainly sold at Auction. Should a lending body have the unpleasant task of repossessing a property from a non-paying owner, they then must use their best endeavours to get as much as possible for that property or risk being sued by that owner for underselling the property. Most lending bodies instruct an agent to conduct a Public Auction for the property but do not allow any reference to the fact that it is a repossessed property. However, once a contract is issued, the lending body is shown as the owner, so it's not hard to detect.

Logically, there is no scientific way to assess the value of a property. All properties are individual and each one is unique. Even a standard Company home is completely unique by the very land it sits on! So yes, comparisons can be made to properties already sold within a certain radius of an individual home and certainly this is what all agents and Property Valuers take into account when assessing a realistic market price.

However, the aesthetic of a home can add considerable value to a property – and one that cannot be quantified. There are people that have a great flair for home décor and certainly with all the TV programs on home improvement today, this is big business. Like with most forms of art, the average person 'knows what they like', but they may not be imaginative or capable of being creative within the family home. To employ someone to give a home a makeover can cost literally tens of thousands of dollars, and you have to be prepared to live with a mess for a while. So when a property comes on the market with all this done, it is going to be head and shoulders above its competition. So why should that owner take the first offer put to him? Why should he not really see what the marketplace is prepared to pay?

Under any of these above circumstances I would strongly urge a vendor to Auction his property. As a real estate agent and as an Auctioneer, I am bound to work in the vendors' best interests. If I consider that a vendor will greatly benefit by selling through the auction system, then I am going to highly encourage him to do so and I am going to guide him throughout the whole process. That's my job!

But an Auction cannot be successful without willing participation – that's you! If you are avoiding Auction listings like the plague, you could be missing out on some of the best stock on the market. It doesn't mean you have to overpay for a property – in fact you may be surprised that by being Auction savvy you might end up with your dream home at a fair price.

Most importantly, most lending bodies will more often than not take the result of a Public Auction as a current valuation. We are currently in an upwardly moving marketplace and often Property Valuers that are not frequently in a particular market area are using out-of-date information of sale prices to determine a property's value, or they are being instructed by the banks to do so. They are working off comparable settled sales that may have happened quite a while ago. Consequently, we are seeing buyers lose out on what they want if a Property Valuer comes in at a low assessment.

I have recently had a purchaser agree to a purchase price of $740,000 on a large property in one of my local suburbs. An inexperienced valuer went through this property and assessed its value at $670,000! Fortunately the buyer did not accept this valuation and instructed his broker to change banks. The new valuer came in at $740,000! How can there be a variance of $70,000 between valuers? I don't know, I can't answer this, but there is nothing more frustrating for purchasers and vendors alike. An Auction can solve this problem for both parties.

So, with all this in mind, you can now understand why so many owners are choosing this method of sale. It's not because they are greedy. It is because it is by far the most secure method of making a sale. If you genuinely want or need to sell your home, you need that hammer to come down. The price is often secondary in an owner's considerations. So remember this when you disregard an Auction listing because you wrongly believe that you will end up paying too much for the home.

TIPS FROM THIS CHAPTER:

1. Owners choosing to sell through the Auction system are usually far more committed than through the Private Treaty system

2. These owners are not just driven by price, but are the most likely to need a result

3. You have more time through an Auction Campaign to keep going back and inspecting the property

CHAPTER 2

WHY BUY AT AUCTION?

Looking for a home is an arduous task. When you are on the hunt, you will spend a huge amount of time scoping out properties. Gone are the days when buyers spent almost every weekend being shown homes they never wanted to look at by inexperienced real estate agents, thanks to the internet, but there is still a lot of time spent on inspecting properties on your short list.

What is even more frustrating is when you select the one you like, you go back to the agent that showed it to you and it has been snapped up. Today you are having to make hard and fast decisions; otherwise, the property won't be there tomorrow, and you might regret that. What is worse is when you do see a property you like but by the time you contact the agent it's already gone and you never got a look in, and that keeps happening to you. You end up wondering if you are ever going to find that home!

Up until now you have done everything in your power to stay away from those dreaded auctions! You will even have avoided going to an open house unless there is a price tag on the property. You want a definite price to work off; without this you feel incredibly uncomfortable and vulnerable to being 'had'! But with the auction system, you at least know that the property is going to have a several week campaign, the norm is four weeks, and this will give you time to look at other stock, compare and come back to this one.

Or you could simply "HATE" auctions because you can't get what you want when you want it! Let's face it, we are living in what I call an "instant coffee" society. You are probably extremely time challenged and don't want to disturb the patterns of your life to wait for an auction. You want to be able to walk into a house, make a decision, get it at the price you want to pay for it (you are such a reasonable person, after all) flash the plastic and move on. You do this with everything else you buy, surely you should be able to do this with your next home?

Or you want to be able to slowly make your decision, inspect the property several times, bring in third party experts/family to gaze at the possibilities with you and take on board all their criticisms, savour the idea of living there and then gradually bring yourself to taking action. You are now being deprived of this because you are having to compete with others for what you want, and in your world this simply isn't fair. Gone are the days where vendors are having to smile stoically whilst their home is being scrutinized, praying that you will be the one to make them an offer!

First of all know this: the majority of Auction vendors are far more committed to making a sale happen than the average Private Treaty seller. They have just invested an amount of money to enable an auction campaign to take place. They certainly wouldn't do this if they were half-hearted about selling. So selling by this method isn't just about the money – it's about getting a result. This is definitely a plus for you.

All you really have to do is have the courage to attend the auction and bid according to your budget. Hopefully your budget and the owner's reserve price are in synch. The hammer then comes down on your bid and your purchase is now safe and secure, which doesn't always happen with a private treaty sale.

If you manage to secure a private treaty sale and you lock the owner in to a cooling-off period, you are still vulnerable. Should an unconditional loan approval letter not be available at the end of a cooling-off contract, legal advisors will tell you not to put down the balance of the 10% deposit but to request an extension to the cooling-off period. It is at this point that the vendor regains control of the sale and can refuse to give you extra time. He is within his rights to pocket your deposit and not sell the property to you. So you are left with a very hard choice: forfeit the deposit and the property or take a massive risk, put down the 10% deposit and just hope the loan approval comes through. If it doesn't – you've just lost your 10% deposit.

I have met several buyers that have been through this scenario a few times and have lost several deposits along the way. Either their loan didn't come through in time, or they found a problem with the building reports or they simply changed their mind about buying because something better came along. Add all these deposits up and you could have wasted several thousands of dollars.

With an Auction, no money changes hands until the sale is made. With a private treaty purchase, if you don't sign a contract the property isn't off the market to you and by the time you get your reports done, or your loan approved, someone else may have locked in the owner and you miss out.

The benefit of Auction over For Sale by Tender is simply that you don't know what the rest of the field is doing. You may really want the property, but without open bidding you may either dramatically overbid for the property, or you may lose the property because someone else has dramatically overbid for the property! At least at an auction you know what you have to do to secure a purchase.

And remember what I said about bank valuers? They can be as flawed as anyone else and can dramatically under assess the property which prevents you from getting the loan. No loan, no purchase! The auction sale will help prevent this.

The art to purchasing at auction is being prepared. Hopefully the following chapters will clue you in on what to do, how to do it and how to end up with the property you want at the price you can afford.

TIPS FROM THIS CHAPTER:

1. No money changes hands with an Auction listing unless or until you are the buyer, so you won't be losing anything if you don't buy

2. A typical Auction campaign lasts for four weeks, four consecutive open houses take place and the Auction is usually conducted after the fourth open house. This gives you opportunity to go and look at other stock and come back to this one if you want to buy it. You can also organise a private viewing with the agent at another convenient time prior to the Auction so that you can look at the home more thoroughly

3. The owners going to Auction are usually more committed to selling than the Private Treaty owners and are more likely to need to sell

4. Remember the clearance rates! Not all properties sell under the hammer, in fact statistically around Australia today, 41.7% are getting passed in. That gives you a 28.5% chance that no one else wants to buy at the owner's price!

CHAPTER 3

GETTING YOUR MONEY READY

As an Auctioneer, it is not my role to concern myself whatsoever with your financial position. If you are over 18, not obviously intoxicated and you are registered to bid (more about that later), then I shall be taking your bid. It is not up to me to find out if you have put yourself in a very dangerous position.

So, first things first – get your finances looked at! Really, before you even start looking at houses at all you need to know what you can spend and it doesn't have to cost anything to do this. Just remember if that hammer comes down at Auction - you've bought! There's no cooling-off period. So if you haven't got a pre-approval – you stand to lose up to TEN PERCENT of the purchase price!!

In dollar terms? Well if the average price of a home across Sydney right now is roughly $600,000, that's $60,000 you have just done cold. The equivalent to a year's income for the average person, after tax, squandered because you didn't do your homework.

Any major bank or lending body will be more than happy to have one of their loan officers sit down with you and work out what you can really afford. Gone are the days where you can hope for 100% or 95% borrowings (unless you have other assets that can prop up your new one). There are also an amazing number of independent brokers out there that will happily come to your home at your convenience and inform you of your buying power.

Be upfront with these people. Don't disguise reality. Tell them about your credit cards; personal loans; car loans; living expenses; family maintenance orders etc. Don't leave anything out or it could bite you later. Remember, with an auction you won't be putting in your formal loan application until you've bought, so the last thing you need is to have a Pre-Approval based on fiction and when the time really comes to apply for the loan, you're $100,000 short!

As a general rule of thumb, you need at least 10% of the purchase price and have to show a savings history. You also need to have sufficient funds to pay Stamp Duty, which is payable prior to settlement, and legal costs. Borrow any more than 80% of the purchase price and you will also have to pay Mortgage Insurance. That can often be factored into your overall borrowings, but in some instances, may not.

If you currently own a home and you want to buy before you sell, then enquire about a Relocation Loan. This is a short-term loan which will allow you to borrow 100% of the purchase price and additional costs provided that you have sufficient equity in your current property and have a good, solid income. When this loan is being assessed, consideration will be given for a rental return for either the home you live in or the home you are buying. This will help your borrowing power.

Whatever your position get good financial advice!

The following is an absolutely true story:

I was sitting in my office one day when my receptionist buzzed me to see if I could take a buyer enquiry. As a pretty busy business owner, I was last port of call for buyers, but all the staff were out that day so I was more than happy to see these people.

Within moments, a family of five very large adults were standing at my desk, looming over me from lofty heights; Mum, Dad, two sons and a daughter. All of them declined to sit when offered chairs. They were very agitated and wanted action immediately. I noticed that Dad was clutching a local paper in his hand with the page opened to our ads and with one particular home circled several times in red pen.

"Want to see this house now!" he declared excitedly.

I could instantly see that English wasn't his prime language, so I tried to keep my questions to him simple.

"That's OK, Sir" I responded. "Why do you want this house so much?"

"My youngest daughter go to High School round corner and can walk from here. We go NOW!" he demanded.

So far, so good, but being an old hand in the real estate market at this time, I wasn't going to break my protocol of asking qualifying questions before I got him in my car and showed him the house.

"I'll soon take you out there, Sir, but before I do that I have to do my job properly and ask you a few questions. First of all I need to take your names and a telephone number." I said, not allowing myself to be intimidated by their sizes, impatience or excitement.

They huffed and puffed as they gave me this information, obviously put out that I was wasting so much valuable time on trifles.

"Will you be paying cash for this house, or have you got a pre-approval from a Bank for your loan?" I persisted.

"Not go to bank yet, but no problem for money!" The father answered in a raised voice, now moving from foot to foot because he was so keen to get going.

"That's Ok, I know what the bank will ask, so I will ask some similar questions." I responded, still not allowing them to intimidate me.

They all looked at each other confused.

"We go see house now?" More of a request than a command this time.

"Sir, with respect, before we go into anyone else's house I need to find out if you are in a position to buy. So, where do you work and who will be buying the house?"

"We don't go to work. But still can afford house!" The father replied, indignantly.

I wasn't completely put off; I had seen instances at that time in the marketplace where unemployed people had gotten loans, but I didn't really fancy their chances. It would all depend on how much of their own money they were putting towards the purchase.

 "That's OK Sir, so how much deposit do you have to buy this house?" I enquired.

Nodding that he understood the question, the father pulled out a piece of paper from his jacket pocket with a flourish.

"$50,000!" he proudly declared, unfolding the new piece of paper and pushing it towards me across my desk.

I looked at the paper and, with all the self-control I could muster, held back from bursting out laughing. The paper he had just put in front of me was typical bait advertising 'subscribe to this and go into a draw to win ....' And at the bottom of the page was a replica of a cheque for $50,000! This was their deposit.

Now imagine if the property was an Auction property and these people had unwittingly rolled up on the day, registered and then proceeded to be the successful bidders....

As the Auctioneer, I would have still been paid my fee for calling the Auction (and I would be cracking up laughing as I left the premises!). As a real estate agent, I would be running after the under bidder to grab him before he left the premises. As the owner, I would have gone from a super-high to feeling like I had just been crash tackled and wanting to take on whoever was responsible for this folly. As the buyer, I have just put myself in the position of being bankrupted by the vendor.

So now you understand why getting your finances checked out is so important.

TIPS FROM THIS CHAPTER:

1. Get a pre-approved loan or professional advice for the amount of money you can borrow before you go house hunting

2. Be totally open with your financial commitments – hold nothing back or it could bite you later

3. If you find a property that you like, go back to your lender and seek their advice that you are in a position to attend and bid at Auction

4. TAKE NO CHANCES! This can cost you almost your year's income and result in you losing any hope of buying a property at all

CHAPTER 4

DOING YOUR HOMEWORK

Ok, so now you know what you can afford and you are keen to buy. You've scoured all the real estate internet sites and some of the local papers and you've seen a few houses with prices on them that are in your price range. You also see a beautiful home that ticks all the boxes for what you need, but it's going to Auction. What do you do next?

Well, let's get real here. If the two properties with the right price tags are significantly inferior to the one going to Auction, then you shouldn't expect to be able to afford it – common sense should tell you that. But go and look at it anyway! Why? Because you will be learning from the experience and because if you are a typical buyer you

CAN afford it, you just don't want to borrow so much money.

Nine times out of ten, buyers are told what they can borrow but they don't want to go anywhere near their maximum. That isn't necessarily a bad thing, but if you buy something inferior, chances are you will be moving again within the next few years. That's great for us agents – another commission to be made and another Auctioneer's fee to be paid – but every time you sell and buy a house here in NSW, you are throwing away the turnaround costs of AT LEAST $40,000 or significantly more in commission, stamp duty and expenses. Sometimes it is better to go to a higher figure now and get what you are really happy with and stay there longer, rather than throwing away that kind of money.

More often than not, the agent looking after the listing will be holding an open house and you have an open invitation to go to that property at that time. With some of the more exclusive homes, you will have to be well qualified by an agent before you are given permission to attend an open house, so I will focus on the lower end of the market, which is where we find the least knowledgeable and majority of buyers.

If you are going to an open house, be prepared to give the agent your name, address, telephone number and email address. If you don't want to give this information, then some agents – like me – won't let you into the property. We have a duty to protect the current owners' property, and things can go missing! Also, would you like it if you opened your home to the public and anyone was let through the door? I don't think so.

When I put my first home on the market in Australia some 25 years ago, I chose not to sell the house myself – I didn't work in the area where I lived at that stage and I wanted distance between myself and the buyer – so I gave the listing agent my keys and they showed my home whilst I worked. I didn't realise how creeped out I was going to feel when I got home to find all these calling cards on my breakfast bar meaning that I'd had several inspections through the day. Total strangers had walked through my inner sanctum – seeing exactly how I lived – and I had no idea who they were! Had the agent coupled that with *"I didn't take their details, they wouldn't give them to me"* I would have sacked him on the spot.

I promise you a good agent is far too busy to hassle you just because he has your details. But he will be contacting you again to get your opinion of the property and to ask if he can put you into his database for future listings. Isn't getting in first on a new listing better than always finding out about a property after someone else has bought it?

And please, don't walk into an occupied home and start opening cupboards or taking photos. If the property is tenanted, they will hate that and may make it almost impossible for us to show the property ever again. If the owner lives there, he won't want dozens of people milling through his home opening and closing cupboard doors. Do this at a personal, individual inspection if you like the home and are keen to buy. And remember to ask permission first. I actually lost a listing once because a buyer helped herself and opened a built in wardrobe that revealed the vendor's stash of hardcore porno movies! The buyer screamed (she had children with her), the vendor ran in and then ran out red faced! The property came off the market the next day. I learned very quickly from this lesson, I can tell you! Remember, this is someone's home; show them some respect.

Now you're at the property, what do you look for? There are basically two distinctly different buyers: those who want to live in the property and those who want an investment. The former are more emotional (or should be!) in their decision processes and the latter should really just buy from the wallet.

Let's talk about the emotional buyer or EB first. You are looking for your next family home, which will be so different from when you bought your first house. Back then, you just felt grateful that you were buying a house at all! You didn't have high expectations; you always knew that this was a stepping stone and one day you would be getting your dream home. But now you've lived there for a while and you have a growing family, the time has come to move. Your experience of living in this home has taught you all the things you truly want in your home – it's taught you this because chances are you have lived without them up until now!

So you will have a list of 'must haves'. Some will be more important to you than others. For example, you cannot live without air conditioning or an ensuite bathroom. The houses you are seeing in your price range have one but not the other. Which one do you sacrifice? Just remember, air conditioning can be added but it is far harder, or almost impossible to add an ensuite. Or will a three way bathroom with access from the main bedroom suffice, provided that you get ducted air conditioning?

Or you may really want a double garage. The houses you're seeing are with single garages. Can you put a second one on? How much do you really need that second garage? Can you get what you want in your price range, or should you look at either increasing your borrowings or look for a property that has all these benefits but is poorly presented or much older? You can always improve on the look of a property at a later date when you are a little more solvent.

You may not be upgrading your home, but you may instead elect to upgrade your location. You've lived in a lovely home out in the Suburbs but now you want to live closer to the City. Unless you are in a position to add quite a substantial amount of money to the figure you sell your own home for, or elect to have large borrowings if the bank allows, then you will certainly have to sacrifice some of the niceties you have been used to in order to achieve this. And most definitely if you are buying closer to the City, you will find that the majority of fresh stock is coming onto the market as an Auction listing.

How does the property feel to you? Do you have a good vibe as you walk through? Can you see yourself living there? Most homes will not tick all the boxes for sure, but how much tweaking will need to be done to get this exactly the way you want it to be?

"Size Does Matter! Colour schemes don't!" Or you may elect to go solely on appearances and compromise on other features – your choice entirely. What do you prefer? A bigger home in need of TLC or something smaller with nothing to spend? Your money your choice. But be careful if you fall in love – this can cost you on the day of the Auction! (And I shouldn't be telling you that, for sure!).

Now let's talk about the Investor or Wallet Buyer (WB!). You should be thinking exactly the opposite of the above! The very first thing you should think is *'what will I own in 20 years' time?'*! You will not be living in the property, so you don't have to like it. If you buy on appearance only, then you are simply providing a good looking home for a tenant who may initially pay a little bit more to live in that kind of quality today, but as the home ages and dates, so will the aesthetic, and the rent return will dip. And unless you are willing to continually refresh the property as you would with your own home, then that aspect will gradually fade away. What will you be left with?

The main factors that should interest a Wallet Buyer are:

- Realistic rent return today;

- Vacancy factor;

- Potential for capital growth.

Realistic Rent Return Today

Obviously if a property is appealing in its look, it will attract a tenant quickly at a decent return. Right now we are looking at approximately an average of 5% gross return. But to keep this during your ownership you need to factor in good maintenance of the property. Therefore when you go looking for a property, you need to check out the durability of the property and its inclusions. Timber and tile flooring will have a longer lifespan than carpeting, for example.

Kitchens and bathrooms are the most expensive areas of a property and are usually the most susceptible to fashion. You don't need these to be fashionable, but they do need to be durable. Timber kitchens will normally last longer than laminate and can be sanded back and repolished rather than replaced; older solid bathrooms may not have an eye appeal, but also could be more durable. Good ventilation is also important in both areas – you don't want a problem with mould. Are there any 'risk' areas, such as low balconies on units, glass doors without visual markings, steps that can be tripped up or down? I think by now you get my drift?

Vacancy Factor

The best investment property is the one that is continually occupied, so if the property is in decent condition, the next thing to look for is the location. How close is it to schools, shops and transport? The more central the property, the less likely you will suffer an empty house.

Potential For Capital Growth

What really increases in value in terms of a property? The Land! That really is the prime ingredient in raising a property's value. Land size and shape should be number one on your list to look at. Level or slightly elevated blocks with a regular shape are by far the best blocks to buy. Personally, I prefer an old house on a good block than a young flashy property on a tiny/irregular block any day. As far as strata properties go, well what will you own in 20 years' time? An aging property with additional quarterly costs or a beaut block of land with a house than can be bulldozed if necessary?

So, with these thoughts in mind we go on to the most frequently asked question of all time …….

TIPS FROM THIS CHAPTER:

1. Be prepared to give your essential details to the agent before you are allowed into a property

2. Don't open cupboards doors or take photos without seeking permission first

3. Don't be unrealistic in your expectations with an Auction property. If it is head and shoulders above homes with the right price tag for you, then chances are you can't afford it

4. Weigh up your options: do you buy what you want but go to the higher level of your borrowing power, or do you compromise because of this and resign yourself to an inferior property, bearing in mind that you will probably have to move again within a few years? (Take into account the eventual cost of this)

5. Create your own personal "Must Have" list, but prioritise this. Work out what you may have to forfeit to

stay within your budget or be prepared to increase your budget if you can

6. If you are an Investor, don't "buy with your eyes". Remember you are not going to live there and aesthetics can either wear out or cost you to keep refreshing them. Also keep an eye out for any dangerous aspects to a property: you don't want a tenant to injure themselves and end up suing you

CHAPTER 5

WHAT WILL THE OWNER TAKE?

One of the main reasons owners take a property to Auction is that they want to get the very best price they can out of the market, and they believe that competitive bidding will achieve this. Sometimes they are right, sometimes not. Like buyers in reverse, owners will have three prices in their heads: their "dream" price (well over their expectations), their "fair" price (well, in reality, this is what it's worth) and their "Ouch!" price ("if that's all I get, I don't think I'll bother selling!").

Most agents do not want to know the reserve price before the last week of the Auction, and even if they get that the moment they sign up the listing, they will not be telling anyone what it is.

As an Auctioneer, the NSW law states that I must have that reserve price in writing before the Auction starts or I cannot call the Auction. But that is for my eyes only.

In some instances, I can't even tell the Listing Agent what it is! I've even called Auctions where the owners have specifically told me NOT to say *"It's on the market"* when reserve price is reached!

So, *"What will the Owner Take?"* Every agent I know handles this differently. Sometimes you will be given an Opening Bid – that's where the Auctioneer will start on the day; it bears no relationship to the reserve price, but is usually set 10% to 20% below the reserve price, or the owner's ideal sale price. What it will show prospective buyers is that if you were hoping to get the property for less than this, don't waste your time, you've got no chance. And don't confuse this with the Reserve Price, it is simply a guideline.

What I hate (and I'm sure you do too) is the practice of some agents that totally mislead buyers into believing that the house will sell way under reasonable market value. They seem to think by getting dozens of buyers to the property on the day of the auction, the price will get pushed up or the vendor will crack. Either way, this isn't working in the vendor's best interests, which is the golden rule that we are supposed to work by. If you are told a price by an agent that sounds too good to be true, it probably is! Again, use your common sense! Compare the property with other homes that have sold or are being marketed at a price, and draw your own conclusion.

A good agent will quote other sale prices to you to give you a guideline. Bear in mind, every property is unique, and there can be a variance between properties. Also, if you are in a mobile market, that is, if prices have been rising in the past few months, then there's a chance you will have to pay a little bit more than recent results.

Some agents will give you a price guide, which is something like *"we're expecting this to sell for over ....."* How much over remains to be seen, and won't be determined before the actual Auction date.

There has only been one instance in my almost 30 year history in real estate that I handled this question completely differently. Back in the late 80's, I listed a property that I assessed to be worth approximately $100,000 to $110,000 (those were the days!). The owner was completely committed to relocate to Townsville and told me that he would happily accept $95,000 for the property. Working in his best interests, I suggested that he Auction the property, and that he give me permission to market the property with the heading "Reserve Price set at $95,000". He was quite happy to do this.

I ran a four week campaign with this heading and was totally swamped with enquiries and inspections on the home. Back then the Franchise Group I belonged to insisted that all Auctions were conducted in rooms and on the evening of this Auction the room was packed.

Immediately prior to the Auction starting the owner came up to me and said:

"Maria, I had a brilliant dream last night! I dreamt that the hammer came down at $115,000 and I was ecstatic!"

Well the hammer did come down that night, but not at $115,000. It came down at $137,000! And I received the most beautiful bouquet of flowers the next day.

The truth of the matter is – we often do not know what the owner will take! This figure can totally vary from listing the property to the actual auction date. Owners, like buyers, are fluid. They can change their minds for a variety of reasons, and they can end up taking less than they originally planned or they can want more. If their circumstances change during the Auction campaign, this can have a significant influence one way or the other. For example, if they find a property they want to buy themselves, then their need to sell can become more acute and they can become more flexible with their price. Conversely, if they miss the property they want to buy, they can raise the price so that they only sell if they get considerably more than market value.

So, like a typical agent and Auctioneer … I haven't answered your most frequently asked question!

However, this now leads me on to the second most frequently asked question …..

Can I buy before Auction?

There are instances where the property absolutely must go all the way to Auction, and this is usual with sales that are Mortgagee in Possession, Deceased Estates that are being handled by the Public Trustee, and situations where there is conflict between parties owning the property. The agent will tell you this when you first ask this question.

However if there is an opportunity to buy before auction, get one thing in your head right now. If you buy before

Auction, you MUST submit an excellent price for the owner to cancel everything and sell to you. This price MUST be close or MUST hit the Owner's Dream Price to stand a chance.

Think about it. If you were the owner and you had just spent, in some cases, several thousand dollars on a marketing campaign, still have to pay an Auctioneer anyway (the majority of Auctioneers will get paid once they are booked – if they are Auctioneers only then they totally rely on this income to survive and they have to work on a tight schedule – particularly on a Saturday), have had quite a large number of people go through your home already, why would you drop everything to sell at anything other than your Dream Price?

So, if this is the home you want, make a great offer. Don't think you can go backwards and forwards pitching for the property - make a good, solid upfront offer to show you mean business.

When buying before Auction, you must put down the ten percent deposit (this may be negotiable) and you must (in NSW) get your solicitor to sign a 66w certificate which eliminates a cooling-off period. This will vary from State to State, Country to Country. But wherever you are, the principle of purchasing prior to auction is to make it a definite sale without any further chance of pulling out unless you sacrifice your ten percent deposit.

What you have to weigh up, of course, is how will the owners respond? That really will depend on the level of activity on the property, and you can see this yourself at the open house. If the owner accepts your offer, you've bought. If he doesn't – don't give up!

I've listed many auctions where there have been good offers prior to an Auction which the owners have refused to accept that have then sold to the same buyers for less money than originally offered. Conversely, I have also seen properties sell for far more money than offered and to the same buyer. There is no definite guideline. It's all a game of chance, but you have to be in it to win it.

The other aspect of buying prior to Auction is the timing. If you are looking at the property in the first few days of it coming on the market, your chance of buying before Auction is far higher than in the last week of the campaign. But also remember to gauge the agent's response: usually if an agent is urging you to buy before auction, it could mean that there is not a great deal of competition on this property – it may be in your best interests to wait!

Each property owner will respond completely differently to this question depending on their personal circumstances. However, it is highly unlikely they will sell before Auction unless they are presented with an offer that is just too good to refuse. So if you have the funds to pay an exceptional price, then certainly you have a good chance. But if you want to buy before Auction at a mediocre figure, expect to be knocked back. That doesn't mean that you won't get what you want at Auction though! So don't give up!

Other questions you need to ask about the property

Probably the most important question you can ask about the property is "why are the owners selling?" This is hugely critical when it comes to what the owner is likely to do on Auction day.

If an owner has an acute need to sell, he will be more likely to listen to the offers he gets prior to the Auction and set his reserve price accordingly, or, if no offers are forthcoming, he will be very realistic in his expectations. He may like to get more, but he won't necessarily hold out for his Dream Price on the day. A definite sale may be far more important to him. So this is a question you really do need answered.

Should an owner be selling because he has already bought something else, the agent will reveal this. However, if an owner is selling because of a separation, divorce or financial difficulties, this will not (or should not!) be revealed. Some owners are happy to be transparent – they just want the place sold as quickly as possible and at the highest price, so they may be willing for an ad to read "Beat the Bank!" or something similar, but this is their prerogative and not up to an agent to disclose if the owner requests this.

Or the property could be an investment property where the owner has decided for whatever reason to cash it in. He has heard that the market is hot, so he's happy for the capital growth and now decides to sell. This can mean that his selling needs are not so acute and he may be more likely to hold out for a Dream Price or he will simply hold on to the property. Under these circumstances, the agent may tell you that the sale is for ROA reasons – Realisation of Assets. This type of property may be tenanted at the time it goes onto the market and the agent must base the inspection times around the tenants' willingness to allow inspections.

With this type of sale, the property may be subject to an existing lease, which could mean that you are buying a property with a tenant until the statutory time frame for that tenant to move out expires. Or if you are an Investor, this could be ideal. You buy a property and you also enjoy an income from the first day of ownership. A lease should be attached to the Contract. Yet another reason for you to get this document examined by your solicitor.

Often the agent will work the owners' motivation into the heading or text of the advertising, so do look out for this, and when you inspect the property do make this one of the questions you make sure you ask. Motivation has a significant impact on the vendors' decisions on Auction day. We do occasionally get owners that will only sell *"if they get their price"* but these owners are more likely to sell by Private Treaty rather than Auction because they don't want to incur too many costs if the property doesn't reach their Dream Price.

With a Deceased Estate however, the reasons for selling are absolutely obvious. Until the properties of an Estate are liquidated, they are a liability rather than an asset to the beneficiaries. Grass still needs to be cut; rates have to be paid; empty properties can be liable to vandalism etc. So the beneficiaries are more than likely to be willing to sell on the day of the Auction. However, there may be a strong sentimental attachment to the property. Their loved ones lived here. They may have grown up in the home and are having difficulties in parting with it, in letting go of the past. They may want to make sure that they honour their loved ones' memory by pushing for the very best price. So don't be surprised if the expectations of beneficiaries are high – but often they will come to terms with market value and sell on the day. The only other problem there might be with a Deceased Estate is if a beneficiary challenges a Will after an exchanged contract. This could drag out settlement time. Your legal advisor will more than happily explain consequences to you if you ask him.

TIPS FROM THIS CHAPTER:

1. Nothing is set in concrete with an Auction listing. The reserve price is usually set immediately prior to Auction day and can vary for a variety of reasons

2. Don't expect to get a straight answer out of any agent. It is there job to encourage buyers to attend an Auction and compete for the property. It is their duty to work in the best interests of the Vendor, and getting the owner his top dollar is their mission

3. You will be given a guideline of sorts for what the property may sell for, but use your own common sense when you compare it to other properties out there

4. There are circumstances where buying before Auction is not possible, it depends on who is doing the selling

5. Don't expect to buy before Auction at your dream price – if you really do want to buy before the day, make your best offer to seduce the owner before the auction

6. If this doesn't work – don't give up! Many an owner has knocked back a superb offer before an auction and regretted after the auction

7. If the owner says "Yes" then secure the sale as quickly as possible. The property will not come off the market until a sale is unconditionally secured

8. Make sure you ask the agent what is the motivation of the vendor

9. Read the ad thoroughly – the answer may be here

10. Take into account the answer; this information can be useful in assessing what the owner will do on the day of the Auction

11. Make sure you ask your legal advisor questions pertinent to this answer, i.e. if you purchase a Deceased Estate what can happen

CHAPTER 6

GETTING READY FOR AUCTION DAY

Right, so you are going to bid at an Auction, what do you need to do?

You've already checked out your finances and you are good to go. The next most important step is to get the Contract for Sale checked out by your solicitor or Conveyancer.

Make sure you know what the terms and conditions are and let someone who is legally trained look at the Contract for Sale. You don't want to find out after you've bought that the property is subject to road widening, flood affected etc. etc.

All you have to do is request a copy of the Contract from the listing agent, who will be more than happy to email, post, or give you this document. This is his way of gauging the interest in the property.

Your solicitor will advise you of anything deemed to be detrimental, or unusual in the contract. He will also be able to, if necessary, change terms that he is not happy with by consulting with the solicitor that prepared the contract on behalf of the vendor. This is the only way these terms can be changed. It is not the responsibility of the selling agent to go through this with you.

Terms and Conditions of a Contract can change immediately prior to an Auction by the owners' solicitor or Conveyancer. Should this occur, I will read out the new terms, but I will not be explaining them! Unless an agent or Auctioneer is legally trained, he should not be giving you legal advice at all. Be aware of this!

"CAVEAT EMPTOR! - BUYER BEWARE!"

This is the golden rule of Auction. It is up to the buyer to do any necessary reports on the property; it is not up to the vendor to provide them. I used to believe that owners should supply these reports until I heard of an incident where the owner was related to the selling agent and they had bodgied up a pest report that covered up a pest problem.

One thing I stress over and over again to buyers is **GET A PEST REPORT DONE!!!** Here in Australia, we have a problem with White Ants (termites) that can infest a property unbeknown to an owner, and can have eaten through a lot of timber work in a property without being detected by the untrained eye. In severe cases, these pests can cause so much damage that the house has to be pulled down!

Several years ago, we were appointed as selling agents for a property that was repossessed by a lending body and we were instructed to take this property to auction. On the surface it looked like any other house in the street, was relatively well presented and was only a few years old. Thank goodness it didn't attract a lot of interest and didn't sell under the hammer, because immediately after the auction the only party interested in the property, who couldn't bid at auction, did a Pest Report and the house was riddled with termites! They still bought the home – at a radically reduced price – but they didn't get saddled with a lemon unwittingly!

I have handled literally hundreds if not thousands of properties over the years through the Auction process – yet I can still count on one hand the number of people that have listened to my advice and actually obtained a pest report. ARE YOU SERIOUS? The consequences can be absolutely dire. And this can all be avoided by spending just a few hundred dollars. Unfortunately the thinking of most buyers is *"I could spend this money but not end up with the property if someone outbids me."* That's true. But personally I would prefer to waste a few hundred dollars on a report and know that the property is safe rather than get stuck with a home that could cost me thousands more to fix up a problem I didn't know existed.

This might really surprise you, but I was a human being before I became a Real Estate Agent and Auctioneer. As a human being, even if I make money from a sale, I take absolutely no pleasure in selling a problem to anyone. **SO GET THAT REPORT!**

Another thing you need to know, as a Real Estate Agent I do not need to disclose that someone died in a property unless it was as a result of a violent act (in which case this must be recorded in the Contract for Sale) or unless I AM ASKED!!

So if you really have a hang up about a property being a Deceased Estate, ask the agent where the previous owner passed away. He is under obligation of disclosure to tell you once asked. He is under obligation to the owners not to advertise this fact.

Finally, work out what you are willing to pay. Have similar figures to the vendor, only in reverse!

- **'Dream Price'** – what you would love to get it for.

- **'Fair Price'** – reality compared to what else you've seen in the marketplace with similar benefits; and

- **'Ouch Price'** – YOUR LIMIT!

Your limit is personal to you. It is based on what you can afford, how much you like the property and how it suits your needs. Discuss this with your partner well prior to the auction. Waiting until the Auction is actually being called can cost you the property! I, like most Auctioneers, will wait for a buyer to bid, but not to a ridiculous extent! I've waited and waited for buyers, with the other bidder seething that I am taking so long, and then had no choice but to drop the gavel. I then have the buyer that missed out complain because he missed the property! Being prepared means that this won't happen to you.

In some instances, buyers actually organise a valuer to go through the property. This can give you a useful guideline, but again, with an Auction, nothing is definite. The actual sale price at auction will be determined by the bidders and absolutely no one can foresee this. Let's face it, everyone's taste is different. The adage *beauty is in the eye of the beholder* is most appropriate when it comes to the family home.

If you are most keen on a property and you are fortunate enough to have seen the property at the first open house, then attend the subsequent open houses. By doing this, you will gauge the property's popularity. Even so, I have had properties that have had over fifty inspections prior to the Auction and yet on the day of the Auction, only a handful of buyers have registered!

The most important suggestion I can make is **ATTEND THE AUCTION**! Synchronicity is an amazing thing ... if it's meant to be it will be.

One other thing that is most important: get your deposit money ready for the day of the Auction, because if you don't, even if you are the successful bidder, the owner can still refuse to sell the property to you.

More often than not, Auctions are called on site on a Saturday or on a Thursday evening in rooms when all banking facilities are closed. Therefore you need to prepare beforehand if you don't have a personal cheque account. Many people don't want the expense of purchasing a bank cheque unless they are the buyer and so they arrange through the agent with the owner that on the day/night of the Auction they will pay a largish amount of cash (say up to $5,000) and then bring the full deposit to that agency by a certain time the following banking day.

However, it is preferable to make this request the day before the Auction because otherwise if the vendor doesn't agree, you need to make alternative arrangements. If you leave the request until the day of the Auction, like I said, the owner can refuse to sell you the property.

If you are concerned about not knowing the exact amount you need to make a bank cheque for, I suggest that you use a "rounded" amount and get an arrangement to make up the difference. For example, if you are expecting the property to sell for over $700,000 then bring a bank cheque for $70,000 and have an arrangement that you can top up the deposit the next banking day. I have to say nothing breaks my heart more as an Auctioneer than if I see a bank cheque made out for $75,000, say, and the property sells for $745,000! (Doesn't happen often, I might add!).

We also need to get the owners' permission to accept a Deposit Guarantee Bond prior to the Auction. Bank transfers after the Auction are acceptable, again, provided that permission from the Vendor has been sought.

As far as exchanging on less than 10%, again, this request needs to be made before the day of the Auction. I have called many auctions where the bank has repossessed the property and in many instances they are most particular that the deposit has to be paid according to the contract. I explained this all the way through the marketing of one particular property, even to the extent of writing this on the leaflets that were handed out, but, even so, a buyer turned up on the day, was successful in bidding for the property but only had a 5% deposit. Needless to say, the bank representative refused to accept this buyer and we sold to the under bidder.

If you have a personal cheque account, don't forget to transfer the necessary funds into this account! In NSW, the law states that agents have to bank all monies receipted within 24 hours, or the next banking day. For example, if the Auction is on a Saturday and the Monday is a bank holiday, the funds must be banked by end of trade on Tuesday. On an ordinary Saturday then the deposit must be banked by end of day Monday.

If the funds aren't in the account and your cheque bounces, then you are in breach of the contract and can lose the property and even be sued!

Finally, if you are intending to be an absentee bidder, or you wish to have someone bid on your behalf, you must register for the Auction prior to the Auction time. For example, if you are working and you want another member of your family or your legal representative or even a real estate agent to bid for you, you must make sure that you are registered and that you have signed a written authority nominating your representative to bid on your behalf. You will have to show your I.D. at the point of registering and then your representative will have to register on the day of the auction and give the Auctioneer a copy of that written Authority, before the start of the Auction.

If the person you are purchasing the property with is attending the auction and will be bidding, there is no need to do this. Only one partner needs to register. However, if you are not in a position to attend the auction immediately after the sale occurs, you will also need to give the Auctioneer an authority to sign the contract on your behalf.

TIPS FROM THIS CHAPTER:

1. Take a copy of the Contract to your legal advisor to get his advice

2. Confirm your borrowing power with your lending body

3. Get a Pest Report done, particularly if a property is looking tired and worn

4. Organise your 10% deposit by either personal cheque or bank cheque – no cash please

5. If you need to organise your deposit for a lesser amount or payment by a different method, make sure you get the owners' permission well in advance of the Auction day, preferably through your solicitor in writing

6. If you want certain terms of the vendors' contract changed, make sure you get your solicitor to get this in writing also

7. Organise your I.D. And don't forget to bring it with you on the day

8. If you want someone to bid on your behalf, make sure that you also organise their I.D. and sign an Authority to allow them to bid on your behalf

9. If you want to be an absentee bidder make sure your are registered any time before the Auction. You can do this in an agent's office or at one of the last open houses and that you nominate who will be bidding for you. Give them an Authority to bring to the Auction

10. If you are an absentee bidder get permission from the owner as to when you will be signing the Contract. Again, submit this in writing and get their consent in writing.

CHAPTER 7

AUCTION DAY

This is it! You are at the property, or the Auction venue, what should you expect to happen?

Registering to Bid

First of all, if you wish to bid at an Auction in NSW, you need to register. You need to have I.D. that will show your current place of residence and a photo of yourself if you are the bidder. If you are electing to have someone else bid for you, both your name and I.D. and the I.D. of the person bidding for you need to be registered. You also have to give the Auctioneer an Authority that this person is bidding on your behalf. The ideal I.D. is a current Drivers Licence. If you don't have one, then a utility bill with your name and current address plus some form of photo I.D. is acceptable – maybe a club membership card, or your passport?

Here in NSW, if you do not hold a Drivers Licence you may obtain a voluntary Photocard to prove your identity. These are available from the Roads & Maritime Services, your local RTA office.

If you are buying the property with a partner, such as spouse, parent, sibling etc. then only one of you need to register, not all parties. However, all parties do need to sign the contract if you are the successful bidders.

Just remember, you do not have to bid just because you have registered, but you certainly cannot bid if you are not registered! Auctioneers can be fined thousands of dollars if they accept a bid from an unregistered bidder! They don't make this mistake, I can assure you!

Once registered, you will be given a number. This number is exclusive to you and must be shown every time you make your bid. Every Auctioneer in NSW today has an assistant recording each bid – it is a legal requirement. The bids are recorded by writing down the number of the bidder and the amount he has bid. If you don't show your number, you may get overlooked, particularly if the Auction is fairly fast-paced.

I was calling an Auction one time and I had several bidders in front of me. The bidding was fairly spirited and it was mainly between two contenders. At the end of the Auction, I summoned the gentleman whose bid was the final bid over to the table to sign the contract. A young lady stepped up and claimed "That last bid was my bid! I bought the property!" I checked the register and the bid recorded was the gentleman's. I firmly told her that the bid had landed on him – it was his property. She became very indignant and argued with me. She hadn't made a bid up to that point; the gentleman who had been bidding all the way through was standing immediately behind her and held his card up at each bid.

Like most Auctioneers, when I have bidders regularly bidding at an auction, I am always going to look back at them between bids. If there is a new contender, they have to make sure I see them! Being shy can mean you don't buy! The lady that contested the property was hers didn't make me aware of her bid – she never held up her number. I simply didn't see her, and she didn't help herself. The gentleman bought the property.

Auction Warning Signs

When you attend an auction, whether on site or in rooms, the Auction Warning Signs must be on display. In some States, they need to be on display for a specific amount of time, but whatever the local State rules, they must be on display prior to the start of the Auction.

Some Auctioneers read out these rules, some don't. Personally, I do and the reason I do this is because I know I work in an area where English is the second language to most people, and even though they may be fluent in speaking English, this does not necessarily mean they can read English.

I will now go through rules that apply in NSW individually, with an explanation for each point:

The Auctioneer must have the Reserve Price in writing prior to the commencement of the Auction.

This is self-explanatory. If I don't have this, I don't call an Auction. I have had owners tell me on several occasions to "just call the Auction – I'll let you know if I'm selling". No, sorry, no can do. I am not risking my licence on an instruction that is contrary to the law.

The reserve price that the owner sets can move down during an Auction, but never up. From an Auctioneer's point of view, I prefer a realistic Reserve Price which is gauged from buyer feedback during the Auction campaign. However, many owners like to inflate the reserve price so that they can make their final decision on what they will take as the Auction is actually being called. This may mean that I have to stop the Auction and consult with the Vendor if the bidding stops before the Reserve Price is reached.

The Vendor is allowed one Vendor Bid only. If this bid is used, the Auctioneer must announce in a clear and precise manner that this bid is on behalf of a Vendor.

Personally I don't like using a Vendor Bid because this is usually the death knell of an Auction, but on occasions I will use it, provided that I can also state that the next bid will be the buying bid. That is up to the Vendor. I will discuss the use of a Vendor Bid prior to the Auction and I will usually set this with each Vendor as a fall-back position if I need to use it.

The highest bidder is deemed to be the purchaser, subject to the reserve price.

Again, self-explanatory. If the property is 'On the market' this means that the reserve price has been reached and if the bidding stops at any point thereafter and you are the final bidder, you've just bought yourself a house! So now go and sign the Contract!

In the event of a disputed bid, the auctioneer is the sole arbitrator and the auctioneer's decision shall be final.

I'm the boss, baby! So like I said before, if one person claims a bid was theirs, I can over-rule this. I can also refuse to accept a bid which I deem is not in the best interest of the Vendor. What does this mean? Well, if a bidder appears to be intoxicated I will not take his bid (so don't have a few nips for courage before an Auction).

Also, I can set the pace of the Auction by refusing small bids that are far away from market value or the reserve price. For example: if a property has a reserve price of $600,000 and a bidder opens at $400,000, I will then call for a bid of say $420,000 or $450,000 immediately after. If someone bids $401,000, I can refuse that. I will set the increments that I wish to raise the bidding. I will advise about the strategy of bidding generally later on.

A bidder is taken to be a principal unless before bidding the bidder has given to the auctioneer a copy of a written authority to bid for or on behalf of another person.

There are a number of excellent Solicitors and Conveyancers out there that will attend an Auction with their clients – make use of this if you are nervous and really want this property. However, should you bring someone to the Auction to bid on your behalf, register yourself, register your nominated bidder, and give the Auctioneer something in writing signed by you to state that you want this person to bid for you.

If you cannot attend the Auction on Auction day, you can still bid by telephone. To do this you need to register (which can be done any time prior to the Auction date) and you can nominate a real estate agent or friend to bid on your behalf with you on the other end of the phone, giving them instructions. Again, your nominated bidder will also have to register, but it will still be you signing the contract, and you can make arrangements with the agent and the owner when this can be done.

A bid cannot be accepted after the fall of the hammer.

An Auctioneer can be fined several thousands of dollars if they accept a bid once the hammer comes down, so don't leave it til the last minute to make your bid! I often have bidders trying to play cat and mouse with me – why, I'll never know! But they leave it right up until I am at the third and final call before they make their move. Sometimes they delay too long, the hammer lands, they lose! (And so does the owner!).

Have a lengthy discussion with whoever you are buying with or who is advising you BEFORE the Auction regarding your "Ouch!" price. Don't leave it until the Auction is happening to do this. Like I said before, I will give some time to bidders to make a decision, but not a ridiculously long time. I actually prefer when a bidder shakes his head that he won't go any further rather than be left in limbo, so if you don't want to bid any more, let me know.

As soon as practicable, after the fall of the hammer, the purchaser is to sign the agreement for sale.

If you are the successful bidder, you will be escorted to a table to then sign the contract and pay the agreed deposit. Don't at that point tell the agent or the Auctioneer that you have bought the property on behalf of your son/daughter/the milkman! You will still have to sign the contract. You may be allowed to put your name down with 'or Nominee' with you signing the contract on the spot, or the owner may instruct the agent to sell to the under bidder, not you. But be aware that if you do elect to sign with 'or Nominee' you may be up for two lots of stamp duty here in NSW! Check this out with your legal advisor.

At every Auction I call, I also announce the deposit rule, which is:

Unless before bidding the bidder has been granted a request by the vendor to place less than 10% deposit on the day, the vendor can refuse to sell the bidder the property.

Although I have already dealt with this, I will go over it again:

If you are the successful bidder, your options to pay the deposit are either by personal cheque, bank cheque or Deposit Guarantee Bond. I have had bidders turn up to Auctions with plastic bags full of cash, I have to say, but in this day and age I would refuse to accept large sums of cash – it leaves us way too vulnerable to theft.

Most agencies are only insured for a limited amount of cash stolen (approximately $2,000 per day) so if we take possession of tens of thousands of dollars, we are liable and responsible for that money until it is banked! One agent I know had a deposit of $80,000 stolen from the person doing the banking in the middle of the High Street in the middle of the day! And he had to cover this loss himself!!

The other disadvantage of taking wads of cash are that we then have to sit and count it – not a time friendly activity if we are calling another Auction straight after this one! So please, no cash.

Again, I've said this before but I want to emphasize that the absolute best advice I can give you is take a copy of the contract to your legal advisor well beforehand and let him/her do their job. They will contact the vendors' solicitor and will get permission or adjustments made on your behalf.

TIPS FROM THIS CHAPTER:

1. Register to bid, whether you decide to bid or not. If you are not registered, you definitely cannot bid

2. Be familiar with the Conditions of purchasing at Auction.

3. Make sure you have thoroughly discussed your "Ouch" price with the person you are buying the property with. Don't take too long to make your bids or you could miss out

4. When bidding, hold up your allotted number and call your bid out loudly and clearly

5. Be guided by the increments that the Auctioneer is calling for, but you can call out larger bids should you wish

6. Make sure you have your deposit with you on the day, or have had permission granted to exchange any other way with any other method PRIOR to the start of the Auction

CHAPTER 8

STARTING & BIDDING AT AUCTION

With on-site auctions

When the property is marketed there will be a time as well as a date that the auction will commence. With in-rooms auctions there will be a venue and a general time advertised, but the 'Order of Sale' for the properties may not be available before that evening.

On-site Auctions are usually started promptly at the time advertised, although there could be a delay for whatever reason. A buyer may be stuck in traffic and phone ahead and request that the Auctioneer delay proceedings and wait for them, or even the Auctioneer may be running late if they too get caught in traffic and are running between auctions. Whatever the reasons, there could be a delay, but usually that would only be for a few minutes.

In-rooms Auctions,

These auctions however, will usually start very promptly. If there are several properties on the Auction block on the same night, the Auctioneer must be very conscious of the time to get through all the stock. I have called over twenty auctions in one night, and, as the proceedings started at 7pm and the hall closed at 11.30pm promptly, I had to make sure I got through all the stock very efficiently.

When creating an 'Order for Sale' for in-room auctions, most agencies will select their most popular properties to begin the evening and to end the evening. The preferable order is to have the first three properties to sell to set the mood for the evening, then in the middle have the least popular and then to keep the absolutely most popular property for the last auction. We want to keep the crowd in the room!

So if you see that the property you are after is either first or last on the list for the night, expect some competition. If the property you are keen on is situated in the middle, you may not have too hard a job to buy it.

With in-room auctions there is usually a video played of each house prior to the auctioneer making reference to the contract. I have attended many in-room auctions where buyers that have missed out on a previous property start bidding on a property just from these slides! In fact, I have sold literally dozens of properties in-rooms sight unseen. It's amusing that when buyers get in the mood to buy, they will do this!

I have also had many on-site auctions where a buyer has turned up on the day of the auction, never seen the house before, and has registered, bid and won the property. Obviously to do this they must be financially well prepared and have a great deal of confidence in the marketplace.

Bidding at Auction.

First of all, do yourself a favour, if you are a first-time auction buyer, go to any auction before the auction date of the property you want to buy and just be an observer in the crowd. This will help you enormously. Or watch many of the auction shows that are currently on the television or YouTube to get an idea of what to expect.

So now we are right at the point of bidding – every buyer and seller's nightmare time when the stomach muscles (and others!) are clenched hard – let the battle begin!

At every Auction I call, I may have a preamble about market conditions, I read out the terms and conditions of purchasing at auction, I talk a little bit about the Contract and a little bit about the property and then I call for an opening bid…… there then usually follows a period of dead silence with everyone waiting for everyone else to make a move!

What are you going to do? So many bidders think that the strategy of waiting for others to bid first is clever – well sometimes it is and sometimes it isn't.

I think one of the most successful purchases I have ever seen was when a bidder started the bidding high, right on the reserve price in actual fact (although he didn't know this), and scared the competition off so much the hammer came down before anyone else could collect their wits! A great strategy.

If an "opening bid" or "bidding starting from…" has been advertised, then the Auctioneer will start the bidding by asking for that figure. If there have been no indicators, the Auctioneer is obliged to start at the figure that any registered bidder calls out, with increasing bids following. This is called *"An English Auction"* or an *"open ascending price auction"*.

As an Auctioneer, this is the style of auction I prefer. I usually start by saying "I'm in your hands for an opening bid…." And I will then wait until some brave person raises their number and gives me a figure. I personally don't care how low the starting figure is, I am only looking for participation at this stage. And the more participation the better so that we can set the tempo of the bidding.

There are still some old school Auctioneers that start by calling for very high bids, and then keep dropping down and down until a bidder starts to bid. This is known as a *"Dutch auction"* or an *"open descending price auction"*. This style of auction was named after its best known example: the Dutch tulip Auctions. Personally, I don't like this method of bidding. I always feel that if we drop down and down and no one bids, then the buyers begin to believe that the field doesn't have confidence in market value and their own opinion gets swayed. I do see a lot of herd mentality at auctions, so I prefer to start low and work up, not the other way round.

Auctioneers will steer an auction by suggesting the increments they want from the bidders, like I explained before. You can often tell how close you are to the reserve price by the amounts the Auctioneer is willing to take. For example, if the bidding starts really low, I may be calling for the next bid to be $50,000 or $20,000 more. Once I get close to reserve I shall then look at taking lower increments, maybe $10,000 or $5,000 bids. When I get within $20,000 of reserve, I could then be calling for bids of $1,000 or $2,000 – sometimes even $500 bids, depending on the strength of the bidders. My job is to get to reserve price, whatever that may be. I will not make a judgement call on market value of the property – that is not my responsibility. Once I reach that reserve figure, I will then allow virtually anything, but I have never been an Auctioneer that will allow increments of under $500. We are selling a property, not cattle!

No matter what I call for, you can bid more than that, but most Auctioneers will not take less.

A good strategy is to make a strong bid at some point – it really will put other bidders off. For example, a couple of weeks ago I was auctioning a property where the bidding opened at $300,000 Before I could call for a counter figure, a contending bidder called out $400,000. At this particular Auction there were over 20 registered bidders, but after that bid only two stayed in – it totally cleared the field!

So my advice to any bidder is to make strong bids. If you make weak little bids, your competition will swamp you. The other advice I would give is when you are bidding and the bidding reaches say $728,000 – don't go to $729,000. You are leaving the door open for someone else to step through! Round your bid off to $730,000. In other words, make sure you have the zero bid – often a buyer will stop at the next zero, so make sure that bid is with you.

Don't have a herd mentality at an auction.

If you have done your own research and you want this property, show it! Don't let other bidders' ambivalence rub off on you. Because if you are watching everyone else and what they are doing, there is a possibility when you do bid that your bid will not be seen, as I mentioned earlier.

As an Auctioneer, I go back and forth between active bidders, I'm not looking for new contenders until the bidding slows down. So if you want to join in, shout your bid out and raise your number so that you will not be overlooked.

When you are competing with fellow bidders, come back hard and fast – it really does put the competition off! I had one gentleman actually say to me, "there's no point in me bidding again, he'll just pay more than me." He then declined to bid and the other guy got the property. When the other gentleman came to our table to sign the contract he said to me "I'm glad he didn't go again, I was on my last bid."!

You really don't know what another person is going to do, you are guessing, so how much do you want this house? Often experienced bidders will out bluff their opponents and win the day.

Another point that may benefit you is, many seasoned bidders wait for the property to be called "On the Market!" before they make their move. But even these veterans of the auction system can be put off by a strong contender. If they are Wallet Buyers – investors, builders, developers etc. – they want to buy anything and everything at the lowest price possible. Seeing a committed buyer will turn them off.

I said earlier to start with a strong bid. I also believe that you should end with strong bids. So often I see small and half-hearted bids towards the tail end of the auction and instead of shaking off the competition, the competition hangs on like a leach! Blow the competition out of the water with a hard strong bid, say $5,000 or $10,000 at the end of the bidding if you really want the property and you can afford to do this! That will soon clear the field.

One strong tip I want to share with you: don't let the competition know what you are thinking! I saw a lady the other day keep shaking her head, then bid again. Her competition knew that she was at the absolute limit of her buying power and knocked her off with a strong bid. Have you ever played a card game? Well winning at cards is often a matter of bluffing, so it can be with auction. Try to remain impassive, stoic and care but not too much! If you do end up shaking your head, mean it!

Notwithstanding all of the above: don't get carried away at an Auction!

Set your limits prior to the event and stick to them. Don't be foolish and get carried away with competing with someone else – more often than not you will win the property, but at what price? This really isn't a contest, so don't treat it like one. You were alive before you ever saw this property and you will remain alive if it doesn't become yours! Chances are there is another home around the corner, or not even on the market yet, that will suit your needs – so don't let the hype of the moment overtake your common sense. That is unless you fall in love, have buckets of cash to fulfil that adulation and can afford to do so. Then, by all means, go for it! It is, after all, your prerogative.

So, when is a property called "On the Market!"?

When the reserve price is reached or exceeded. If the bidding is spirited, I won't call this out until that bidding has slowed down. I am not obligated to reveal that figure to anyone, including the purchaser. Once this is declared, the property is selling regardless of whether another bid is made or not. It is selling and once the bidding stops, the auctioneer will "call" the last bid three times and if there is no further bidding the hammer will come down and the auctioneer will call "SOLD!"

Please understand that the Auctioneer is employed by the owner and the Auctioneer's job is to get the very best price for their owners. On that basis, do not expect the hammer to come down quickly. Even though I am continually badgering for buyers to speed up, I will also play with the time. I will take a sip of water. I may talk about the property's attributes. I may talk and talk to the buyer about making another bid. All these actions are delaying tactics to allow that buyer to make another bid. We may be "On the market" but I want my vendors to know that I have done my absolute best to get the juice out of the marketplace.

If the bidding stops before the Auctioneer calls "It's on the market", …this means that the bidding hasn't reached the reserve price. What will normally happen then is that the agent and or Auctioneer will consult with the owners to see what they want to do. If the owners are willing to sell, the Auctioneer will declare that the property is "On the Market!" which means that the owner has dropped his reserve price and will sell at this last bid price. Sometimes this may then kick the bidding on and other contenders may start bidding again. Otherwise, the Auctioneer has permission to sell at this last bid price.

The agent or the Auctioneer will do their utmost to bring the last bidder and the vendor together before the fall of the hammer. So there could be a lot of work by the agent or the Auctioneer, going back and forth between the last bidder and the seller. If an agreement is made by the two parties, the Auctioneer will state that *"the buyer has increased his offer to ...... and the property is now on the market, I am selling today!"* This doesn't mean that the property has sold, because anyone else can now throw in a bid and sometimes this does happen.

If the vendor is not willing to sell at the price the bidding has stopped at and the buyer will not increase his offer, the Auctioneer will state that if there are no further bids he will *"Pass In"* the property. If this happens, then the last bidder has the first rights to negotiate with the vendor after the Auction and that buyer will still buy under Auction conditions, which means he signs the contract, pays the agreed deposit and the property is sold. If no agreement can be made with this bidder, the agent will then approach any of the other under bidders to see if they are willing to pay a figure that the owner will take. If you are not the last bidder but you still want the property, make sure you have the last bid before the property is passed in, otherwise you will be left out of the negotiations until the first bidder finishes.

So now let us look at what you should do if the last scenario eventuates and you are the last bidder…

TIPS FROM THIS CHAPTER:

1. Be on time. There is nothing worse than rushing things, particularly if they are stressful anyway. If you can't be on time, ring ahead and let the agent know – he is actually there to help you

2. Should the property being auctioned be part of a group of properties in rooms, check the order of sale; you should be issued with this as you go into the rooms. This may give you a guideline to the popularity of the property you are after

3. Are you well prepared enough to bid on another property sight unseen? Do you know the area well enough to know where the property is located? If you don't, then don't get carried away! You may end up buying a property right on a Highway with limited access! (I've seen this done before!)

4. Make strong bids. Often the bidder who starts the auction is the one that gets the property!

5. Don't have a herd mentality and wait to see what other buyers are doing

6. When you do bid, call your bid out loud and raise your bidding number

7. Listen to the increments that the Auctioneer is calling for – you could be closer to the reserve price than you realize

8. Bluff a little! Don't let your opponents know what you're thinking.

9. Don't get carried away with the competition! No matter how badly you want this property, it is not worth you struggling like mad for the next few years because you paid beyond your means. Do you really want to sell your car to make up the difference?!

10. If the property is called "On the Market" it is selling, make your move

11. If the reserve price isn't reached, make sure you are the under bidder and the last bid has landed on you

CHAPTER 9

NEGOTIATING AFTER AUCTION

Let's assume that the bidding for the property doesn't reach the reserve price and the last bid lands on you. As I've explained, at this point in time the agent and the Auctioneer will seek the vendor's instructions. Should the vendor not be willing to sell to you at this price, the agent will then come to you to ask you to increase your bid.

This is a very dangerous time. Should you increase your bid and the Auctioneer then declare "It's on the Market! I'm selling today!" this could encourage other bidders to then join in and spirited bidding could then ensue. This is what I want as an Agent and as an Auctioneer, but it could mean that you, who have done all the work up until this point, have lost the house to another contender or have been forced to pay much more that you wanted to.

One of my clients recently told me that she attended an auction to purchase a property, not with me I hasten to add. Her last bid was $585,000. The agent went backwards and forwards between her and the vendor and told her that if she made one more bid of $1,000, the vendor would put the property on the market. She did as he suggested and bid at $586,000. The Auctioneer then announced that the property was on the market, now selling.

As soon as the Auctioneer said this, a person standing in the crowd who wasn't even registered to bid at this point, indicated that he wanted to bid. The Auctioneer stopped the Auction and gave that person time to register, the new bidder then made a bid of $590,000, which was over what my client was in a position to pay, and he got the property!

There is absolutely nothing wrong with this scenario as both the agent and the Auctioneer are employed by the vendor and must always work in their best interests. So allowing someone to stop the Auction and register is permissible, that is their job. In hindsight my client's best strategy at this point would have been to let the property get passed in and negotiate directly with the vendor immediately after the Auction. In this situation, my client would have bought the house at $586,000 and no one else would have been in a position to outbid her.

Remember, if you are registered at an Auction and the property doesn't sell, you can still buy under Auction conditions up until 12 am that night.

As an Auctioneer and an agent, I much prefer a sale under the hammer. It is usually at the best price for the vendor and it is a done deal. By the same token, be realistic in your expectations as a buyer. Don't expect a $500,000 property to sell for $300,000 just because there are not many bidders at the Auction or because you have just witnessed a property get passed in at a low figure or with no bids. Owners don't have to sell on the day and can wait a little longer for a result.

A few weeks ago, I called an Auction that had six registered bidders and no one made an opening bid. I passed the property in on the day with no bids. The reserve price was $650,000, which was a little too high. That afternoon I had an attendee to the Auction ring me and offer $470,000! Ridiculous! But their mindset was, "well if it didn't sell at the auction and no one made a bid, any offer is a good offer." Not so! That particular buyer didn't buy the property, but I did sell it a few days later for $625,000.

If there isn't a successful sale at Auction or immediately after the auction, the property will then go on the market as a Private Treaty listing. The owner and the agent will take into consideration the market opinion of the property and they will then advertise the property at a price that is normally at the reserve price or very close to the reserve price.

If you like this property but were not in a position to bid at the auction for a variety of reasons, let the agent know that you are willing to negotiate if the property does get passed in. Should this happen, you will purchase the property under a cooling-off contract, not under auction conditions.

TIPS FROM THIS CHAPTER:

1. Be careful about increasing your bid before the hammer comes down! You may have just opened the door again to competitive bidding

2. Remember the last bidder has the first right to negotiate after an auction. Make sure that is you if you want the property

3. If the property is passed in and you are not the under bidder, make sure to inform the agent if you are still interested in the property. You can even make an offer at this stage. If the under bidder doesn't match it, the agent is obliged to come back to you

4. Just because no one else wanted to pay the owner's price doesn't mean the property is going to be discounted by a ridiculous amount

5. If you cannot bid at auction, let the agent know that you are willing to buy after the event. Better still, attend the auction and see what happens. If an agreement cannot be reached with the under bidders, you can make an offer and should it be accepted, you can sign up there and then under a cooling-off contract

CHAPTER 10

WHAT TO DO IF YOU MISSED OUT?

So you missed out on the property. You thought you stood a really good chance at $750,000, but two other people pushed the price up to $780,000, which was well above your buying power. What do you do next?

In a rapidly rising marketplace, it could mean that what you were hoping to get for your money is no longer possible and you really have to think long and hard about this. If this is your second attempt at purchasing at auction and twice you have missed out because other buyers went much higher, I would suggest that you need to start reassessing whether or not you are in the correct price range.

When a market "moves" it does so very speedily, and often a buyer's reluctance to acknowledge this leaves him without a property. What I would do in those circumstances is downgrade my expectations in either the property or the location. I would make do with less at this time, but I would make sure that I get into the market as quickly as possible. Because just like a Tsunami, the prices can take off and leave you well behind extremely quickly. So much so that you cannot save as quick as prices can rise. And you don't want to recognize this when your buying power has diminished even further.

So, instead of looking for a four bedroom home, look at three bedroom homes. Or go back to the drawing board on how many garages do I need? Ensuite or air conditioning? Presentation of the property? Age of the property? Location of the property? It's no good to keep going in the same range of properties and keep getting beaten. Face the facts: you left your run too late. But don't keep doing that because it could get worse! In this type of marketplace the luck, for a change, appears to be favouring the seller. Accept this and lower some of your expectations.

Traditionally, first home buyers would start with something small and simple: a two bedroom unit or a small fibro home for example. Then they would do everything in their power to pay off as much of the mortgage as they could, and look at upgrading at a later stage. Nowadays first home buyers expect to be able to purchase their Dream Home straight off the bat. Like I said before, we are in an "instant coffee" society where we expect to get what we want when we want it! Whether you acknowledge this or not, the market has moved and it will keep moving for some time yet. Accept this and be willing to compromise and you won't be left out in the cold.

Don't blame the Auction system. Auctions didn't drive the prices up: buyers did!

What Happens Next?

Let's presume you were the successful bidder and the hammer came down on your bid. Quite simply it is then that you will be ushered to a table and you will have to sign the Contract or Agreement for Sale and pay the deposit.

At this point, the agent or Auctioneer will write down your details on the front page of the contract together with your solicitor's details. They will also write in the sale price at the appropriate space on the front page of the contract and they will get you to sign this document. If you are buying as a couple, then both of you will have to sign this document. If you are buying as a Company, then a Company Director will have to sign this document. You then have to pay the deposit whichever way you have agreed to do so and you will be issued with a receipt for that.

Once you have signed and paid that deposit, the owners will sign a second contract, if one is available. If for some reason there is only one document, all parties can sign this, although it is not desirable. But anything can happen at an auction. Sometimes a prospective buyer will ask to look at the contract prior to the auction and then inadvertently walk off with it in his pocket. I have to say this has never happened to me, but it can happen and if it does it throws a spanner in the works!

Once all parties have signed the documents and the deposit is paid, both contracts are dated with that day's date. That is it. You have just bought yourself a property! The agent will usually take both contracts with him, do his necessary paperwork and then send your signed contract to the owners' solicitor and their signed contract to your solicitor. You will probably receive a letter in the post the next week from the agent both congratulating you on the transaction and to confirm the amount of money they are holding.

The next working day to this Auction you need to inform your lending body that you have purchased at Auction so they can do their job and finalise your borrowings. Most Contracts in NSW allow 42 days (or six weeks) from the point of exchange until the point of settlement. Settlement occurs when the full amount agreed upon is paid to the owner and you receive keys for the property and can move in at any time thereafter.

Prior to settlement, you are entitled to conduct a final inspection. At that point, you can walk through the property and look for any damage or any missing inclusions that may have happened or been taken after the exchange of the contract. You cannot argue about issues that were like that at the time of the auction - that was up to you to notice - but anything afterwards should be addressed by the vendor. The agent will accompany you on this inspection and will act as witness to the proceedings. Also, you should be able to expect any rubbish to be removed from the site by the owner. Most owners are very obliging and leave their home in immaculate condition, but occasionally we do get some minor issues that need to be addressed, and this can be done through your solicitor at this time. Once this is done, settlement will take place.

Congratulations, you have just bought an auction property! It wasn't that bad, was it?

TIPS FROM THIS CHAPTER:

1. If you keep missing out in a certain price range, then rethink your expectations

2. Go back to the drawing board and reassess the properties you went after and find the common denominator that made them so popular

3. Recognise and accept that you may have missed the boat for this kind of property and rethink what you are prepared to compromise on to buy your next home

4. Change your attitude quickly and by either downsizing the property or downgrading the preferred area, get out there and buy before the market moves even further!

5. You are the successful bidder. You now need to sign the contract and pay the deposit. Make sure you get a receipt or an interim receipt for your deposit.

6. Watch the owner sign the contract and witness both contracts being dated. You can now safely leave the premises/rooms. You are entitled to take the owner's signed contract with you at that point so that you can deliver it to your solicitor. If you don't wish to do this, the agent will attend to it very soon after the auction. It may be useful to be introduced to the owners at this point. Most owners will then open into discussions with you regarding selling furnishings, arranging mutually agreeable whatever and will be willing to talk about the property. You could at this point arrange for a meeting with them to be told how the air conditioner, pool, alarm etc. works and to ask them for any manuals they may have on appliances.

7. The first business day after the successful auction, go to your bank or contact your broker and make your full loan application

8. Simultaneously to the above, contact your solicitor and inform him that you have bought at auction

9. Expect to be allowed to conduct a final inspection before settlement takes place. At this inspection, look out for any damages, or what should have been inclusions being removed. Also check that no rubbish is left on the premises. If you are not happy with anything, contact your solicitor immediately and inform him. He can then either cancel the settlement or make some alternative remunerative arrangement.

SUMMARY

Be prepared! Get your finances looked at and get a pre-approval so that you know what you can afford.

1. Take a copy of the Contract to your solicitor and allow him to go over it and advise you.

2. Get at least a pest report done on the property, get a building report too if you think the property looks like it is run down and there could be hidden problems.

3. Organise your deposit for the day of the Auction. By what method will this be paid and do you need approval prior to the auction by the vendor to accept your deposit?

4. Who will be doing the bidding? If that isn't you, they will need to register and you will also, plus you will need to give them an authority to bid on your behalf.

5. Are you going to be an absentee bidder? Then don't forget to register any time before the auction date – and nominate who will do the bidding for you.

6. Remember when you are bidding to hold up your registered number and call out your bid.

7. Have your plan ready well before you start bidding. What is your "Ouch!" price? What will you do if the property doesn't reach the reserve price?

8. Care, but not too much! You were alive before you saw this property, you will remain alive if this property doesn't end up being yours ... and something else will be around the corner!

GLOSSARY OF TERMS

Agent.

The person acting on behalf of the vendor

Agreement for Sale

Or Contract for Sale. The legal document usually prepared by a legal advisor (solicitor or conveyancer) which must be available before a property can be marketed

Auction

A public sale in which goods or property are sold to the highest bidder

Auctioneer

A person who conducts auctions by accepting bids and declaring goods sold

Bidder

Any person registered to bid at an Auction

Buyer Beware

The Golden Rule of Auction which puts the responsibility on the buyer that if he purchases at Auction, he buys "as is"

Caveat Emptor

The Latin version of above

Deceased Estate

The owner of the property has died and the property is being sold by either the beneficiaries or the Public Trustee

Dutch Auction or open descending price auction

The auctioneer calls for high bids and then drops and drops until a bid is made

English Auction or open ascending price auction –
currently the most popular form of auction.

The Auctioneer begins from a low opening bid and brings the bidding up in increments determined by him/her to the reserve price and possibly beyond

Fall of the Hammer Or hammer comes down.

When the Auctioneer hits the gavel on the table, or anything else, which indicates that the property is sold

Mortgagee in Possession

When the lending body has taken possession from an owner for non-payment of their mortgage

On the Market

The reserve price has been reached and the Auctioneer has the authority to sell the property to the highest bidder

Open House

An allotted time, usually on a Saturday, when the property is open to the Public to inspect without an appointment

Opening Bid

An indication of where bidding will start for a property. This is usually 10-20% under the anticipated reserve price or the owner's ideal sale price

Passed In

The reserve price hasn't been reached and the owner refuses to sell at the last bid price

Registration

It is law in NSW today that all bidders must be registered and to do this they must show photographic I.D. with their Current address to the selling agent, who will then record these details and issue that person with a unique number which must be shown as a bid is made.

Auctioneers can be heavily fined if they take a bid from an unregistered bidder, however this bid is still deemed to be valid

Reserve Price

Usually the least amount the Vendor is willing to take at Auction to allow a sale to ensue. This must be given to the Auctioneer in writing before the start of the Auction

Vendor Bid

A bid made by the Auctioneer on behalf of the Vendor

ABOUT THE AUTHOR

MARIA LAWRANCE

Maria Lawrance started her career in Real Estate in September 1986. She is a Licensed Real Estate Agent and an Accredited Auctioneer, and has won many awards in her career.

Back in 1989, Maria was the first woman in her then Franchise Group to win Salesperson of the Year and she had to beat 86 men to do it! It is an accolade she held for almost twenty years before another lady took that title. She also won Auction lister of the Year in the same year.

Back in 1987, Maria participated in an Auction Listing training course and was one of the first people to introduce the Auction system to her area. Now she has literally thousands of auctions under her belt, both as an Auction lister and as a highly respected Auctioneer. She has Auctioned property all over Sydney and has conducted both on-site auctions and in-room auctions.

Maria sold the last of the three offices she owned in April 2011 with the intention of retiring. Len Pretti, a well-known guru in Property Management, coaxed her to join his businesses. It didn't take much! Maria loves her work.

Even as a veteran of the real estate industry, Maria has some of the best results around. She has just sold her 100th property since joining Len's team two short years ago. Her conversion rate of listings to sales stands at 93%. But she is most proud of her statistic for Agent's opinion to sale price which currently stands at 99.83%! And her average time on market for those 100 sales is 5.2 weeks!

This year alone, Maria has achieved some amazing results for property owners, with her best result being $600,000 over reserve price for one particular property!

She now wants to share her knowledge and her experience with the marketplace to leave a legacy in the industry she has proudly served for over 27 years.

There has never been a book written before to help buyers navigate through the Auction system. But this system also needs you, the buyer. And with the useful tips and hints you will find in these pages, you should now be able to bid with confidence and hopefully win the property of your dreams!

RECENT REVIEWS

MARIA LAWRANCE

Maria's book has given me insight in how to purchase a house through auction.

It is a quick and easy read with great information.

You can tell she really knows what she is talking about and is happy to share the knowledge

Rosemary McCaffrey

This is the good stuff from an expert. I missed out on a bargain house at an auction once, simply by knowing nothing about auctions. And I had a problem selling my own house that took it off the market for 6 months to get rid of an agent who messed up the whole thing. Yes, read it first and you'll be educated. This gets the stars.

Ronald Forbes

This is a great book for anyone thinking of purchasing property or buying property at auction.

I found this to be easy reading and simple enough for the beginner to comprehend all the topics and concepts discussed. I was extremely pleased with the easy to understand material, and guidelines it provided me on the subject.

A straight forward book of valuable knowledge and practical information I can use today.

The great thing about this book is that Maria Lawrance isn't someone trying to get rich selling a get-rich-quick book. Her methods have been proven time and time again, making multi-million dollar investments for many years.

She speaks from real-life experience doing exactly what she writes about.

If you want to invest in real estate, this is a MUST READ.

Christian Bang

As a fellow Real Estate Agent this is a great book, totally enjoyed reading it. Clear and concise it's a must read for anyone thinking of purchasing property. It's a reader's chance to get the inside knowledge on how to embrace purchasing a property at Auction. Highly recommend.

Tracey Wishart

AUCTION
SUCCESS

TOP 10 TIPS TO SUCCESSFULLY BUY PROPERTY @ AUCTION

#1 AMAZON BEST SELLER

LEADING AUSTRALIAN AUCTIONEER & AGENT

MARIA LAWRANCE

ISBN: 9780992417000 (paperback)